WORKBOOK

2

W0018785

TIME ZONES

Carmella Lieske

SECOND EDITION

Australia • Brazil • Japan • Korea • Mexico • Singapore • Spain • United Kingdom • United States

Time Zones Workbook 2
Second Edition

Carmella Lieske

Publisher: Andrew Robinson

Senior Development Editor: Derek Mackrell

Development Editors: Sian Mavor,
   Charlotte Sharman

Director of Global Marketing: Ian Martin

Product Marketing Manager: Anders Bylund

Media Researcher: Leila Hishmeh

Senior Director of Production:
   Michael Burggren

Senior Content Project Manager:
   Tan Jin Hock

Manufacturing Planner:
   Mary Beth Hennebury

Compositor: Cenveo Publisher Services

Cover/Text Design: Creative Director:
   Christopher Roy, Art Director: Scott Baker,
   Senior Designer: Michael Rosenquest

Cover Photo: Calle La Ronda, Quito, Ecuador:
   John Coletti/JAI/Corbis

Copyright © 2016 National Geographic Learning, a part of Cengage Learning

ALL RIGHTS RESERVED. No part of this work covered by the copyright herein may be reproduced, transmitted, stored or used in any form or by any means graphic, electronic, or mechanical, including but not limited to photocopying, recording, scanning, digitizing, taping, Web distribution, information networks, or information storage and retrieval systems, except as permitted under Section 107 or 108 of the 1976 United States Copyright Act, without the prior written permission of the publisher.

For permission to use material from this text or product,
submit all requests online at **cengage.com/permissions**
Further permissions questions can be emailed to
permissionrequest@cengage.com

ISBN-13: 978-1-305-25993-5

National Geographic Learning
20 Channel Center Street
Boston, MA 02210
USA

Cengage Learning is a leading provider of customized learning solutions with employees residing in nearly 40 different countries and sales in more than 125 countries around the world. Find your local representative at:
www.cengage.com

Cengage Learning products are represented in Canada by Nelson Education, Ltd.

Visit National Geographic Learning online at **NGL.Cengage.com**

Visit our corporate website at **www.cengage.com**

Printed in the United States of America
Print Number: 03   Print Year: 2017

Contents

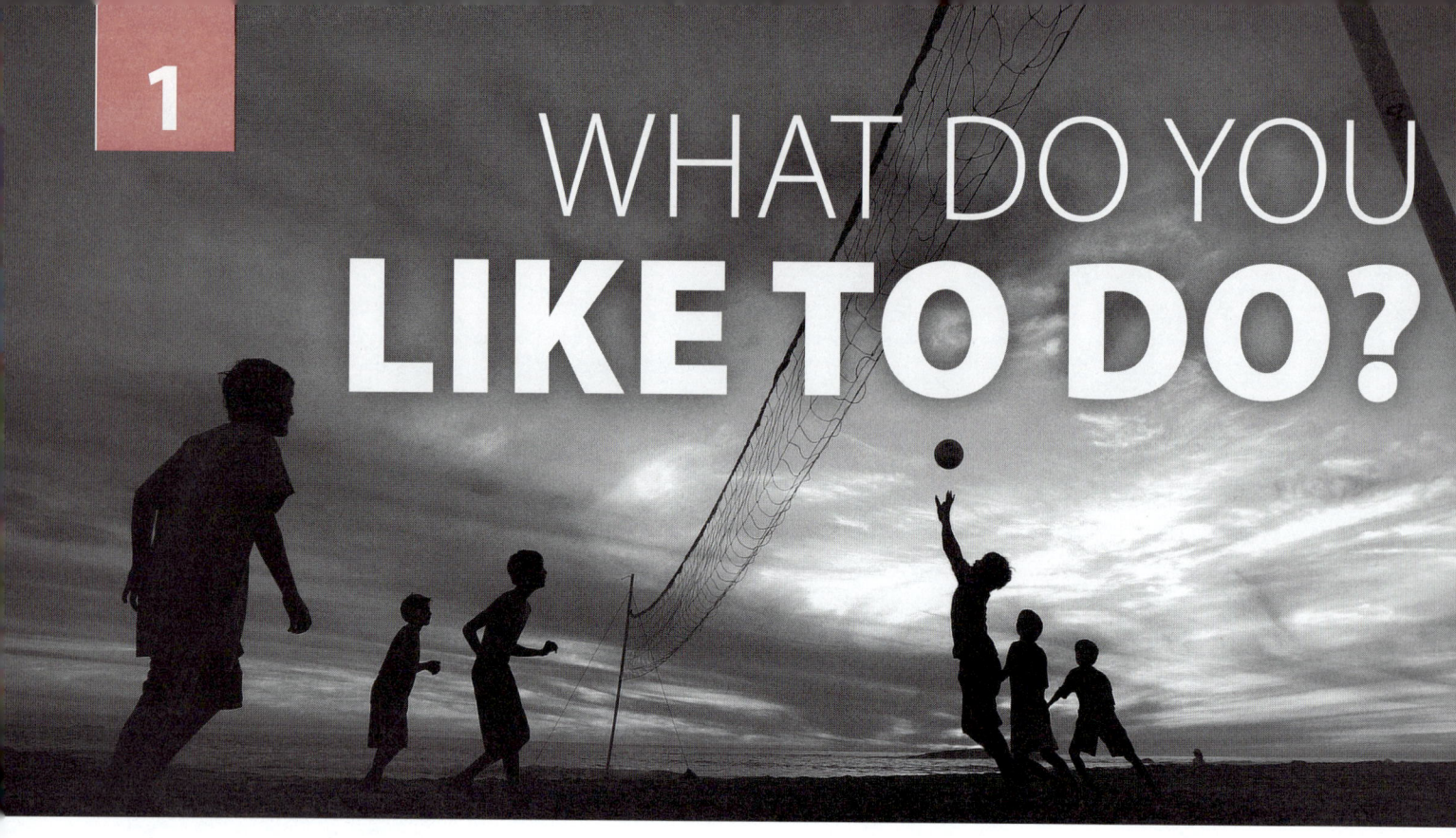

1 WHAT DO YOU LIKE TO DO?

Vocabulary Focus

A **Unscramble the words.** What are the hobbies?

1. s i t n e n _t e n n i s_
2. u i a t r g _ _ _ _ _ _
3. g i n s _ _ _ _
4. w d a r _ _ _ _

5. r a g i o m i _ _ _ _ _ _ _
6. t e k a r a _ _ _ _ _ _
7. c a n e d _ _ _ _ _
8. c o c e s r _ _ _ _ _ _

B **Complete the chart.** Use the words from **A**.

ACTIONS WITH *PLAY*	ACTIONS WITH *DO*	ACTIONS WITH NO OTHER WORD
tennis		

C **Write.** What's your favorite hobby from **A**?

_____

Conversation

Match. Join the correct parts of the conversation.

IN CLASS Practice with a partner.

1. Hi, Susana. Do you like to play sports? ⚬

2. Yeah? What instruments do you play? ⚬

3. Cool! What other things do you like to do? ⚬

4. Really? Me too! Can I see your collection? ⚬

⚬ a. I play the piano, and I can sing.

⚬ b. Sure! I have lots of *X-Men* comics.

⚬ c. Well, I like to collect comics.

⚬ d. Hey, Peter. Mmmm, no, but I like to play music.

Language Focus

A **Complete the conversation.** Circle the correct words.

IN CLASS Practice with two partners.

Jamie: Hey, Dave.

Dave: Hi, Jamie. This is Kelly. (**Do** / **Does**) you want to join our music practice today?

Jamie: Sure! I love to (**play** / **plays**) the guitar. What instrument do you play, Kelly?

Kelly: I (**like** / **like to**) sing.

Jamie: (**How many** / **How often**) do you sing?

Kelly: After school every day. How about you? What do you do after school?

Jamie: Well, sometimes I (**like** / **play**) soccer with my sister. She plays soccer four times a week.

Dave: I like (**to play** / **play**) soccer, too! Our team practices (**every** / **before**) school on Tuesdays. Let's play together!

Jamie: Sounds great!

B **Complete the sentences.** Add the missing word to each question.

1. What do you like to do ~~on~~ weekends?

2. How often you play sports?

3. Do you like collect comic books?

4. How often do you the drums?

5. Do you like to origami?

6. Does she to read?

The Real World

Read the article. Answer the questions.

As a child, JT Smith played lots of board games. Now he's an adult, and he still likes to play games!

Smith changed his hobby into his business. He started a very successful company called The Game Crafter. It helps people make their own board games or playing cards.

On the Game Crafter website, people design and create their own board games. The Game Crafter then makes them, and prints them. It even sells them! Big toy companies sometimes buy the games and sell them in stores around the world.

Smith believes it's possible to follow your dreams and make your hobby into your work. He thinks work can be fun!

1. As a child, JT Smith played lots of games.   T   F

2. Smith's hobby is now his business.   T   F

3. The Game Crafter helps people make their own video games. T   F

4. Toy companies sometimes buy the games and sell them   T   F
   in stores.

5. Smith says that work can be boring.   T   F

Reading

A **Read the article.** It is mainly about _____.

    a. Dylan's hobbies   b. the group Lil' MDGs   c. the Internet

CHANGING THE WORLD

Dylan Mahalingam is a regular American boy. His favorite subjects are math and science. He loves music, and he can play the piano. His hobbies include tennis and basketball. He also likes to swim and snowboard.

Dylan also likes to help people. At nine years old, he and two friends started a non-profit group—Lil' MDGs. They use the Internet to tell young people about education, health, the environment, and other issues around the world.

The group has several goals. One goal is to help people have enough food to eat. Another goal is to help all children go to school. It has helped over one million children around the world so far.

Lil' MDGs now has more than 24,000 members in over 40 countries. It wants to inspire young people to work together, and make the world a better place for everyone.

B **Complete the diagram.** Use information from *Changing the World*.

Favorite School Subjects

1. _____

2. _____

Dylan Mahalingam

Lil' MDGs

Uses the Internet to tell young people about

6. _____, 7. _____,

8. _____, and other issues.

Hobbies

tennis

3. _____

4. _____

5. _____

Two Goals

9. help people have _____

10. help children _____

C **Answer the questions.**

1. Dylan likes many activities. Which ones do you like, too? _____

2. Does your school have a group to help people? _____

Writing

WRITING TIP **Revision: Punctuation**

Most sentences start with a capital letter and end with a period (**.**). Use commas (**,**) to separate words in lists.

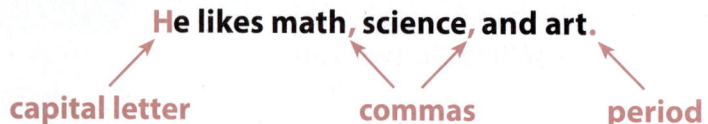

Questions start with a capital letter and end with a question mark (**?**). Sentences with exciting or surprising things end in an exclamation point (**!**).

A **Write sentences.** What are your hobbies and interests?

1. _____

2. _____

3. _____

4. _____

5. _____

B **IN CLASS** **Talk with a partner.** Read your sentences from **A**.

2 WHAT DOES SHE LOOK LIKE?

Vocabulary Focus

A **Match.** Join the correct picture to the description.

1. ○   ○ a. curly   4. ○   ○ d. wavy

2. ○   ○ b. short   5. ○   ○ e. spiky

3. ○   ○ c. braces   6. ○   ○ f. glasses

B **Unscramble the words.** What are the colors?

1. a g y r   _ _ _ _   4. l b c a k   _ _ _ _ _

2. w r n b o   _ _ _ _ _   5. e d r   _ _ _

3. h i w e t   _ _ _ _ _   6. d l o b n   _ _ _ _ _

C **Complete the chart.** Use the words from **A** and **B**.

HAIR STYLE	HAIR COLOR	FACE
		braces

Conversation

Complete the conversation. Put the sentences in the correct order.
[IN CLASS] Practice with a partner.

a. _____ She's tall and has blond hair.

b. _____ Is it long and curly?

c. _____ Mmm . . . I don't know. What does she look like?

d. _1_ Hi Andy, where are you? It's 4 o'clock. I'm at the baseball game.

e. _____ Oh, there she is! Hey . . . umm . . . Are you Andy's sister?

f. _____ No, it's short and straight.

g. _____ Oh, hi, Max. Sorry, I'm late. I'm still on the bus. Is my sister there?

Language Focus

A **Complete the questions and answers.**
[IN CLASS] Practice with a partner.

1. What does Sophie look like? She has long, straight _____.

2. Does Tomas have curly hair? _____.

3. _____? He has spiky hair and braces.

4. What does Amelia look like? She wears _____.

Tomas   Sophie   Daniel   Amelia

B Complete the sentences.

Elena: Hi, Carrie. Do you have this month's *Teen Magazine*? There's a photo of my cousin Ben's band on page 30.

Carrie: No way! What _____ he look like?

Elena: Well, _____ tall, and the band members all _____ short, spiky hair.

Carrie: I found the picture. Which one is Ben? Does he _____ freckles?

Elena: No, that's his friend, Andy. Ben _____ glasses. He _____ braces, too.

Carrie: Uh-huh. Is he _____ a red shirt?

Elena: Yeah. That's him!

Carrie: Cool!

The Real World

Complete the article. Use the words in the box.

> once   apps   brain   languages   improve

Can computer games make you more intelligent? Some scientists believe it's possible to help your (1) _____ to learn new things and work better, even when you're older. There are lots of (2) _____ and computer games designed to test how your brain works, and how to (3) _____ it.

Apps like Lumosity give your brain a workout. Apps like this have games to help improve different skills—like thinking and memory. Other apps, like Duolingo, help you learn new (4) _____. Some games are a race against the clock too, so it's a challenge. According to app developers, using these games just (5) _____ a day for a few minutes helps to improve brain function.

So why don't you try one? It's fun, and it's exercise for the brain!

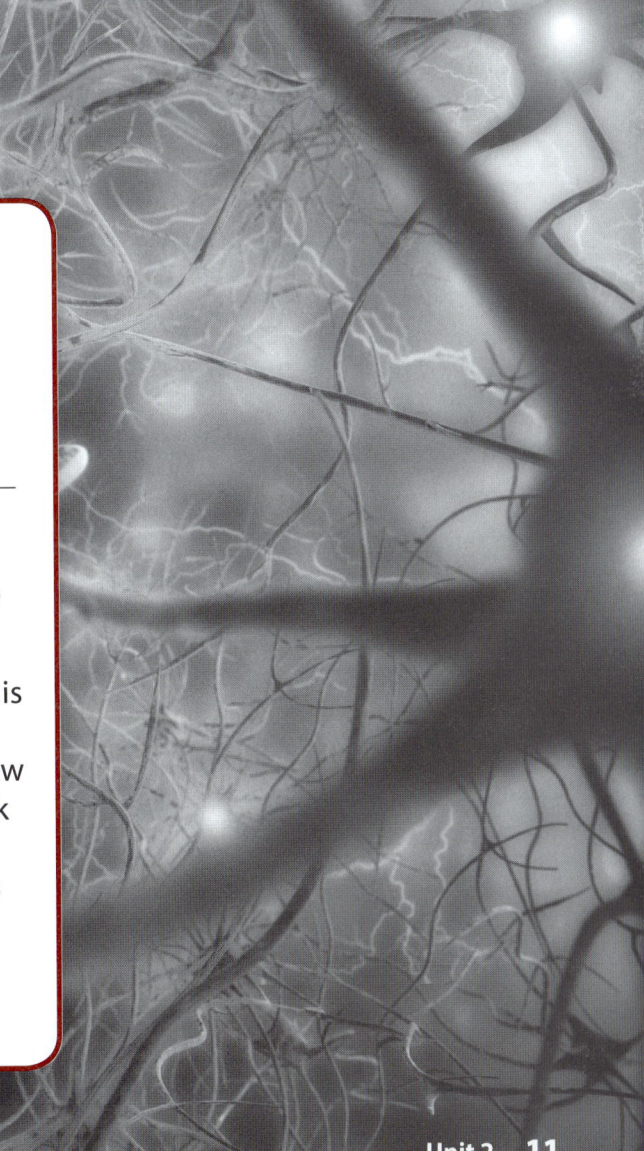

Reading

A **Read the article.** What's another title for this article?

a. Non-Identical Twins   b. The Last Impression   c. Spot the Difference

THE SAME, BUT DIFFERENT?

Identical twins have the same physical appearance. Look at this photo of identical twins—they both have short, straight dark hair, and dark color eyes. They are the same height, and they both wear braces.

On first impression, identical twins look the same, but there are some differences in their looks. Patrick Flynn, a computer scientist from the University of Notre Dame, in the United States, uses computer technology to look closely at identical twins. This technology can see small differences, such as freckles or the shape of the eyes.

The personalities of identical twins can also be different. One twin may be shy, while the other twin may like to talk a lot. Researchers believe that things such as education and the environment can cause these differences as identical twins grow up.

B **Answer the questions on *The Same, But Different?***

1. `Main Idea` Identical twins are twins that _____.

   a. look different   b. look almost the same   c. wear the same clothes

2. `Detail` The boys in the photo have _____ hair.

   a. curly   b. spiky   c. straight

3. `Detail` Flynn uses technology to see differences between identical twins, such as _____.

   a. freckles   b. hairstyles   c. footwear

4. `Vocabulary` Words like "shy," "friendly," and "intelligent" may describe someone's _____.

   a. personality   b. hobbies   c. physical appearance

5. `Inference` According to the article, the environment and _____ can make identical twins different.

   a. school   b. food   c. music

C **Answer the questions.**

1. Do you look like anyone in your family? _____

2. Describe someone in your family. _____

Writing

WRITING TIP Opening greetings (emails)

Use different kinds of greetings to write an email.

	FORMAL	INFORMAL
Emailing someone new	Dear Mr. Smith,	Hi, Chelsea.
	My name is Timothy. Please allow me to introduce myself . . .	I'm Timothy, but call me Tim. I'm 16 years old.
Emailing someone you know	Thank you for talking with me yesterday. It was a pleasure to meet you . . .	How's it going? Long time, no see! . . .

A **Complete the chart.** Write about people you know.

	HEIGHT	HAIR	EYES	FACE
a parent				
a friend				
a teacher				

B **Write an informal email.** Use your answers in **A** and your own ideas to describe someone.

To: Tim   **Subject:** Hi!
_____

Hi! I'm _____. Let me tell you about my _____. _____

name is _____. ____ tall and ____ has _____

hair. In my class, there are _____ students. My best friend is

_____.

What does your best friend look like?

C **IN CLASS** **Talk with a partner.** Read your email in **B**.

I BOUGHT NEW SHOES!

Vocabulary Focus

A Complete the crossword puzzle.

Down

1.
2.
3.
4.
5.

Across

6.
7.
8.
9.

B Circle the correct answer. Which word is different?

1. shorts	jeans	watch	pants
2. hat	skirt	glasses	headphones
3. dress	T-shirt	shirt	sweatshirt
4. sneakers	shoes	socks	backpack

C Write. What items in **A** and **B** do you usually wear every day?

_____

_____

_____

Conversation

Complete the conversation. Put the words in the correct order to make sentences.
IN CLASS Practice with a partner.

Mom: Michelle, are you ready?

Michelle: No! / soccer / can't / I / my / find / uniform

_____.

Mom: It's in your bedroom. the / shirt / door / behind / The / is

_____.

Michelle: Thanks, / but / boots / my / can't / soccer / find / I

_____.

Mom: weekend / The / last / we / bought / ones

_____?

Michelle: Yeah.

Mom: in / car / think / the / they're / I

_____.

Michelle: Thanks, Mom. OK, let's go!

Language Focus

A Complete the conversation. Use the words in the box.
IN CLASS Practice with a partner.

> couple   last   ago   recently   just

Donna: Hi, Linda, I love your jacket! Did you get it _____?

Linda: Thanks, Donna. Yeah, I _____ got it last weekend.

Donna: Cool! My jacket is a _____ of years old. I want a new one.

Linda: Why? It's really nice.

Donna: Well, I bought it two years _____, and brown isn't popular now.

Linda: Really? I think it's great. And I love your purple sneakers, too.

Donna: Thanks. I bought them three days ago—I mean, _____ Friday.

B **Look at the conversation in A on page 15.** Answer the questions.

1. When did Linda get her jacket? _____

2. How old is Donna's jacket? _____

3. Why does Donna want a new jacket? _____

4. What color are Donna's sneakers? _____

5. When did she buy her sneakers? _____

The Real World

Read the article. Complete the chart.

In the United States, about 23% of high school students wear school uniforms. In Japan, almost all students wear a school uniform. So what are the reasons for and against wearing school uniforms?

Some people believe that uniforms help students to focus on school and studying, and not on fashion. They also think that uniforms make all students feel equal. However, other experts believe that students can't show their own style when they wear a school uniform. This stops students from freely expressing themselves. They also think that school uniforms make students less creative.

In January 2015, the U.S. Department of Education studied how teachers feel about school uniforms. Almost all teachers said that wearing a school uniform improved student behavior. No teachers said that school uniforms had a negative effect on students' individuality.

What about schools in your country? Do you wear a school uniform?

REASONS FOR UNIFORMS	REASONS FOR NO UNIFORMS

Reading

A **Read the article.** What's another title for this article?

a. Recycling Glass Bottles   b. Waste Paper Problems   c. Old Trash to New Clothes

PLASTIC **CLOTHING**

Lots of things can be recycled—such as glass, paper, metal, and plastic. Rethink Fabrics is a company based in Seattle, U.S.A. It is trying to fight the planet's plastic waste problem one bottle at a time.

The company's goal is to encourage people to think about where their clothes come from by making clothing from trash. It uses new technology to make clothing items for men and women, like T-shirts.

The T-shirts are made out of 100% recycled polyester (called rPET), from plastic bottles. Inside every T-shirt is a small picture showing how many bottles were recycled to make it, so customers know they are helping the planet. The T-shirts are high-quality and not very expensive to buy.

At the end of the T-shirt's life, the recycling process continues—it is made into another new piece of clothing. Other companies also recycle old clothes into footwear and even household items, like carpets. Recycling your plastic really can help to save the environment!

B **Complete the sentences about *Plastic Clothing*.** Use the words in the box.

> expensive   T-shirts   recycles   trash   help

1. Rethink Fabrics is trying to _____ the planet.

2. The company makes clothes from _____.

3. The company uses plastic bottles to make _____.

4. The clothes are high-quality but not _____ to buy.

5. When the T-shirts are old, Rethink Fabrics _____ them.

C **Answer the questions.**
IN CLASS Talk with a partner.

1. What items do you recycle? _____

2. Would you wear clothes made from recycled plastic? _____

Writing

WRITING TIP Using *because*

Use **because** to join two short sentences.

> **She didn't eat lunch. She's really hungry.**

> **She's really hungry because she didn't eat lunch.**

A **Read the chat room posts.** Write a reply about your favorite outfit.

Message Board

What's your favorite outfit and why?

Posted: 8:55 p.m. by Max   Reply

Hi. My name is Max.
I live in Oslo, Norway. I often wear jeans because it's so cold in my country. I like to wear T-shirts and a jacket with my jeans.

Posted: 8:59 p.m. by Jessie   Reply

My favorite outfit is an old purple and black dress. I love it because it's always in fashion. I usually wear it to parties with high heels.

Posted: 9:05 p.m. by Reena   Reply

Hey, everyone.
I'm Reena. I play a lot of sports, so I often wear shorts, T-shirt, and sneakers. This is my favorite outfit because it's so comfortable.

Posted: 9:15 p.m. by Me   Reply

_____

_____

_____

_____

_____

B **IN CLASS** **Talk with a partner.** Read your reply from **A**.

4 WHAT'S THE COLDEST PLACE ON EARTH?

Vocabulary Focus

A **Complete the puzzle.** Use the chart.

1	2	3	4	5	6	7	8	9	10	11	13	14	15	16
a	c	d	e	i	k	l	m	n	o	r	t	u	v	y

1. $\underline{\text{t}}\ \underline{\text{r}}\ \underline{\text{e}}\ \underline{\text{e}}$
   13 11   4

2. $\underline{}\ \underline{}\ \underline{}\ \underline{}$
   11   15 4 11

3. $\underline{}\ \underline{}\ \underline{}$
   11 10   6

4. $\underline{}\ \underline{}\ \underline{}\ \underline{}\ \underline{}\ \underline{}$
   2 14 7   14 11 4

5. $\underline{}\ \underline{}\ \underline{}\ \underline{}\ \underline{}$
   3 4   4 11 13

6. $\underline{}\ \underline{}\ \underline{}\ \underline{}\ \underline{}\ \underline{}\ \underline{}$
   8   14 9 13 1 5 9

7. $\underline{}\ \underline{}\ \underline{}\ \underline{}\ \underline{}\ \underline{}\ \underline{}\ \underline{}$
   2 10 9 13 5 9 4 9

8. $\underline{}\ \underline{}\ \underline{}\ \underline{}\ \underline{}\ \underline{}$
   2   14 9 13 11 16

B **Complete the chart.** Use the words in the box.

> biggest   hottest   longest   most beautiful   largest
> coldest   tallest   prettiest   shortest   smallest

SIZE	TEMPERATURE	LOOKS

C **Complete the opposites.** Use the words from **B**. You can use them twice.

1. the hottest   _____
2. the tallest   _____
3. the biggest   _____
4. the longest   _____

Conversation

Match. Join the correct parts of the conversation.
IN CLASS Practice with a partner.

1. Hi, Lee. What are you doing?   ○

2. I love geography! I can help you.   ○

3. OK. What's the longest river in the world?   ○

4. Yeah! And where's the hottest desert?   ○

5. That's right! What's the coldest continent in the world?   ○

6. Uh-huh. Last question. Where's the best coffee shop near here?   ○

7. I know, but I'm really thirsty. Let's go get a drink!

○ a. Umm, the Nile?

○ b. Antarctica.

○ c. Oh, hi, Lisa. I'm studying geography.

○ d. Great, thanks! Ask me a question then, please.

○ e. Hey! That's not a geography question!

○ f. Well, I think it's the Sahara. Is it in Africa?

Language Focus

A   **Write.** Use the words to write sentences or questions.
IN CLASS Work with a partner to answer the questions.

1. Who/tall/person/world __Who's the tallest person in the world_____?

2. place/cold/What/world _____?

3. Africa/high/Kilimanjaro/mountain _____.

4. country/world/large/What _____?

5. small/Australia/world/continent _____.

B Correct one mistake in each question.

IN CLASS Talk with a partner. Answer the questions.

1. Who's tallest student in your class?

2. Who's the goodest soccer player in your school?

3. What's the popularest after-school activity in your school?

4. What's the most big store near your house?

5. Where's most beautiful place in your country?

6. What's the famousest food from your country?

The Real World

Complete the article. Use the words in the box.

grow	coldest	plants	warm	long

Reindeer live in some of the (1) _____ places in Europe, Asia, and North America. In North America, reindeer are called caribou, but this is the same species. Reindeer are herbivores, meaning they only eat (2) _____ . They live in big groups called herds. Herds of reindeer often travel over (3) _____ distances—walking more than 2,500 kilometers every year.

Reindeer (4) _____ new antlers every year. Their antlers grow up to 130 centimeters in length! Reindeer live in cold places, so how do they stay warm? One way is that their noses warm the cold air before it travels into their bodies. Their bodies also have lots of hair all the way from their noses to their feet! The hair keeps their bodies (5) _____ against wind and cold.

Reading

A **Look at the photo.** What do you think the article is about?

    a. plants in the desert   b. what a desert is   c. what is in cold places

FULL OF LIFE

When you hear the word "desert," what words do you think of? Many people think of the word "hot." The hottest weather ever recorded, 57°C, was in a desert called Death Valley, U.S.A. However, not all deserts are hot. There are also cold deserts. Antarctica has the largest desert in the world, and it's very cold there.

What other words do you think of? A lot of people say "nothing," or "empty," but this isn't true either. About 15 percent of the world's population live in deserts. There are also insects, birds, and other animals that live there—like snakes and lizards.

So what makes a desert? Well, scientists agree that all deserts are dry. They say a genuine desert gets no more than 25 centimeters of rain or snow a year. This means people, animals, and plants have very little water to drink. They have to learn to live in these extreme places.

B **Read the article *Full of Life*.** Circle **T** for True or **F** for False.

1. Many people think all deserts are hot.	**T**	**F**
2. Antarctica has the world's second biggest desert.	**T**	**F**
3. Only a few people live in deserts.	**T**	**F**
4. There are different kinds of animals living in the desert.	**T**	**F**
5. Deserts get a lot of rain and snow.	**T**	**F**
6. It is easy for people, animals, and plants to live in the desert.	**T**	**F**

C **Write.** Correct the false sentences in **B**.

_____

_____

_____

_____

Writing

WRITING TIP **Using commas to give more information**

Use two commas in the middle of a sentence to give more information.

The hottest weather ever recorded, 57°C, was in a desert.

comma   **comma**

Use one comma at the end of the sentence to give more information.

The hottest weather ever recorded was in a desert, Death Valley.

comma

A **Write a short paragraph about an extreme place.** Give more information and use examples.

_____

_____

_____

_____

_____

_____

_____

_____

B **IN CLASS** **Talk with a partner.** Read your paragraph in **A**.

5

ARE CATS BETTER PETS THAN DOGS?

Vocabulary Focus

A **Match.** Join the opposites.

1. better   2. longer   3. bigger   4. faster
   ○   ○   ○   ○

   ○   ○   ○   ○
a. smaller   b. slower   c. worse   d. shorter

B **Complete the sentences.** Use the words in parentheses.

1. Elephants are (**big**) _____ mice.

2. Dogs are (**friendly**) _____ cats.

3. Dolphins are (**intelligent**) _____ penguins.

4. Rhinos are (**small**) _____ elephants.

5. Sharks are (**dangerous**) _____ dolphins.

C **Write.** Which do you think are cuter, dogs or cats? Why?
IN CLASS Talk with a partner.

_____

_____

_____

Conversation

Complete the conversation. Put the words in the correct order to make sentences.

IN CLASS Practice with a partner.

Hayley: Hi, Tom. Do you want to watch this TV show about animals in the sea?

Tom: favorite / OK, cool! / sea animal / What's your

_____ ?

Hayley: sharks / more interesting / I like / than / because / they're / all the other animals

_____ .

Tom: more intelligent / sharks / Yes, but / are / dolphins / than

_____ .

Hayley: faster—a seadragon / Which / or an octopus / That's true! / do you think / swims

_____ ?

Tom: an octopus / maybe / Hmmm, . . .

_____ .

Hayley: Let's watch the show and find out!

Language Focus

A **Look at the chart.** Complete the questions and answers.

	HEIGHT	MAXIMUM DIVE	WEIGHT	JOURNEY FOR FOOD
Emperor Penguin	About 115 cm	565 m (1,850 feet)	Up to 40 kg	Some walk about 80 km
Adélie Penguin	About 70 cm	175 m (575 feet)	4 to 5.5 kg	Some walk about 50 km

1. _____ The Adélie penguin is shorter.

2. _____ The emperor penguin has a deeper maximum dive.

3. Which penguin is heavier? _____

4. Which penguin has a longer journey to find food? _____

B **Complete the conversations.** Circle the correct words.
IN CLASS Practice with a partner.

1. Tom: Which are (**beautifuler** / **more beautiful**), horses or birds?

   Brian: Hmmm, . . . I guess birds are, but I think horses are (**more interesting** / **interestinger**).

   Tom: Really? Why?

   Brian: Well, horses are (**more intelligent** / **intelligenter**) and (**friendlier** / **more friendly**).

2. Sara: Look at this picture! This baby elephant is (**heavier** / **more heavy**) than my dad!

   Beth: Wow! Is it (**more tall** / **taller**), too?

   Sara: Mmm . . . no. It's only about 1 meter tall.

The Real World

Read the article. Circle **T** for True or **F** for False.

Putty-nosed monkeys live in rain forests in Africa. They make noises to communicate with each other. For example, they make the sound *pyow* when danger is near, and the sound *hack* when danger is coming from the air.

Scientists are studying the communication among putty-nosed monkeys. They believe the monkeys can put sounds together into "sentences," which make new meanings. One "sentence" is *pyow pyow hack hack hack hack*, which means "Let's go somewhere else."

This is a very exciting development in the study of animal communication. Scientists believe this means that some animals are more intelligent than we first thought.

1. Putty-nosed monkeys live in the mountains. **T** **F**

2. They talk to each other with sounds. **T** **F**

3. They make the sound *pyow* when they feel danger. **T** **F**

4. *Pyow pyow hack hack hack hack* means "stay here." **T** **F**

Reading

A **Read the article.** What's another title for this article?

   a. Life in Antarctica   b. Penguins in Australia   c. Summer in Antarctica

ANTARCTICA

Antarctica is colder, drier, and windier than any of the other continents. 98% of the land is ice. Winter starts in June and ends in September, but it's dark and cold for up to seven months of the year. Temperatures drop to -40°C, and the wind speed reaches more than 140 kilometers per hour. This makes it too cold for many animals to stay there during the winter months.

Emperor penguins stay in Antarctica all year round. They are larger than other penguins and are very intelligent. In winter, they spend long periods of time standing in a big circle. This protects them from the cold and wind. The emperor penguins work as a team. They take turns standing on the inside of the circle (where it's warmer), and then on the outside. They never get too cold, even in extreme weather conditions.

B **Answer the questions about *Antarctica*.**

1. Main Idea The article is mainly about weather and _____ in Antarctica.

   a. people   b. seasons   c. animals

2. Inference It is _____ in Antarctica in April.

   a. spring   b. fall   c. winter

3. Detail Emperor penguins are _____ than other penguins.

   a. smaller   b. shorter   c. larger

4. Vocabulary The phrase "work as a team" means _____.

   a. to work as a group   b. to work alone   c. to work as a pair

5. Detail The inside of the circle is _____ the outside.

   a. warmer than   b. colder than   c. the same temperature as

C **Answer the questions.**

1. Which animal is more interesting to you—putty-nosed monkeys or emperor penguins?

   _____

2. Which animal do you think is more intelligent? Why?

   _____

Writing

WRITING TIP **Using parentheses to give more information**

Use parentheses **( )** to give more information.

> **They take turns standing on the inside of the circle (where it's warmer), and then on the outside.**
>
> explains why they stand on the inside of the circle

A **Write a short report.** Use your own ideas to write about an animal you want to see and why. Use parentheses to give more information.

```
|
|
|
|
|
|
|
|
```

B **IN CLASS** **Talk with a partner.** Read your report in **A**.

6

I REALLY LIKE ELECTRONIC MUSIC!

Vocabulary Focus

A **Complete the puzzle to make types of music.**
Look at the picture to help you.

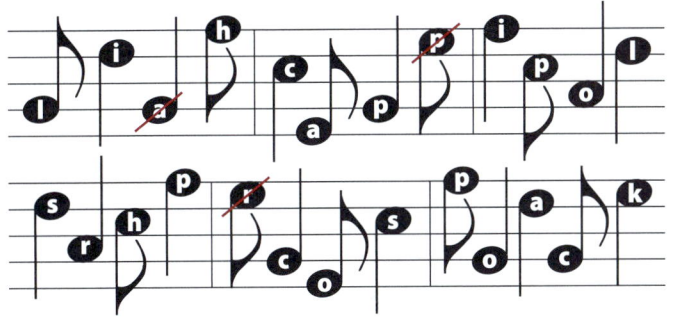

1. r a p

2. _ _ _ _ _ _ _ _ _ _ _

3. _ _ _ _ - _ _ _

4. _ _ _

5. _ _ _ _ _

B **Circle the correct answers.** Which word is different?

1. rock	guitar	pop	hip-hop
2. awesome	amazing	boring	great
3. good	terrible	horrible	bad
4. love	don't like	really like	like a lot
5. can't stand	really don't like	love	really dislike

C **Complete the sentences.** Use the words in the box.

1. ★☆☆☆ I _____ loud music.

2. ★★★☆ I _____ rock music.

3. ★★★★ I _____ to listen to music.

4. ☆☆☆☆ I _____ classical music.

5. ★★☆☆ Rap music is _____.

like	don't like
love	can't stand
OK	

Conversation

Complete the conversation. Put the sentences in the correct order.
IN CLASS Practice with a partner.

a. __1__ I want to buy some music for my sister's birthday. Any ideas?

b. _____ Hmm . . . She loves pop. She listens to One Direction all the time.

c. _____ No problem!

d. _____ Good idea. Thanks!

e. _____ Well, they have a new album coming out next week. What about that?

f. _____ Well, . . . what kind of music does she like?

Language Focus

A **Correct one mistake in each question.**
IN CLASS Talk with a partner. Answer the questions.

1. What kind of music *do* you like best?

2. Which you like better, hip-hop or rock?

3. Who do you like better, Eminem Katy Perry?

4. Do you classical music?

5. Which your best friend like better, electronic music or pop music?

B **Complete the sentences.** Circle the correct words.
IN CLASS Practice with a partner.

Interviewer: I'm at the music festival talking with fans. So, Victoria, (**what** / **who**) kind of music do you like?

Victoria: I like a lot of music, but I like electronic best. Actually, I love (**it** / **them**).

Interviewer: Cool! How about Daft Punk? Do you listen to (**it** / **them**)?

Victoria: They're the (**best** / **better**)!

Interviewer: And (**which** / **who**) singer do you like better, Beyoncé or Taylor Swift?

Victoria: I like (**her** / **them**) both, but I like Taylor Swift better.

The Real World

Marconi Union is a band from England. They recently made a piece of music named "Weightless." Scientists believe it is more relaxing than any other song. The music has a mixture of instruments, natural sounds, and people singing.

The music is eight minutes long. It starts quite fast and then slows down. The rhythm is very important because our heartbeat matches it, and gradually slows down with the music.

As we listen, our brain relaxes. The music slows the heart rate, reduces blood pressure, and lowers levels of stress.

Scientists say the music is more relaxing than a nice cup of tea, a lovely walk, or even a massage!

Read the article. Circle **T** for True or **F** for False.

1. Marconi Union is a singer from England.   **T**   **F**

2. "Weightless" uses more than one   **T**   **F**
    instrument.

3. The song is six minutes long.   **T**   **F**

4. Music can change the speed of our   **T**   **F**
    heartbeat and calm the brain.

Reading

 A **Look at the article.** What's it about?

    a. a singer   b. a composer   c. a guitar player

MAKING **MUSIC**

Ludwig van Beethoven was a world-famous composer, born in 1770 in Germany. But did you know he was deaf?

During his life, he wrote many different pieces of music for orchestras. As well as writing music, he played several instruments, including the piano and the violin.

Beethoven had some famous teachers—like Haydn and Mozart. They all saw his amazing musical abilities from an early age. When he lived in Vienna, Austria, he often played the piano in the homes of very important people.

Unfortunately, he lost his hearing completely by the age of 40.

He continued to play the piano, but it was very difficult for him to hear the higher notes. So, he started to listen to the movement of the lower strings of the piano, instead of listening to the high notes.

Amazingly, he is most famous for some of the pieces of music he wrote after he lost his hearing! Many people around the world continue to play his music.

B **Answer the questions about *Making Music*.**

1. `Detail` Beethoven was born in _____ .

    a. Germany   b. Austria   c. Italy

2. `Inference` Beethoven is famous for his _____ music.

    a. pop   b. classical   c. rock

3. `Vocabulary` The phrase "from an early age" means _____ .

    a. as a child   b. as an adult   c. as an old man

4. `Vocabulary` Another way of saying "he became deaf" is _____ .

    a. he lost his sight   b. he lost his feeling   c. he lost his hearing

5. `Detail` He became completely deaf by the age of _____ .

    a. 20   b. 30   c. 40

C **Answer the questions.**

1. Do you play a musical instrument? _____

2. Have you been to a music concert? _____

Writing

WRITING TIP **Expressing personal opinions**

Use positive and negative language to express your personal opinions.

Positive opinions

> **I really liked . . .**
>
> **I loved . . .**

Negative opinions

> **I didn't like . . .**
>
> **I hated . . .**

A **Read the music video review.** Use your own ideas to write a music video review.

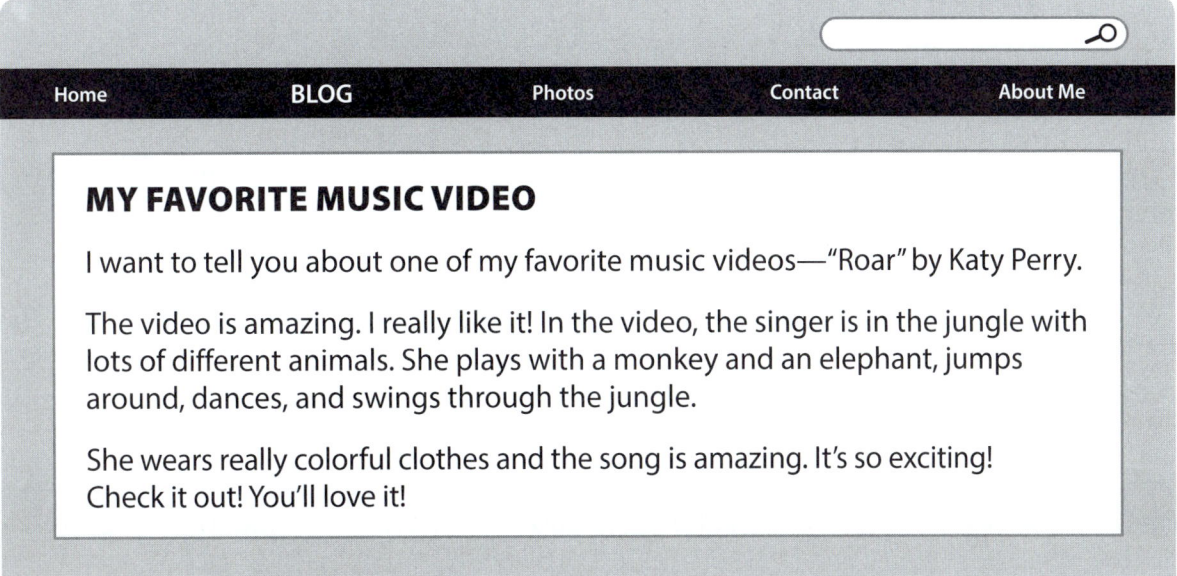

Home   BLOG   Photos   Contact   About Me

MY FAVORITE MUSIC VIDEO

I want to tell you about one of my favorite music videos—"Roar" by Katy Perry.

The video is amazing. I really like it! In the video, the singer is in the jungle with lots of different animals. She plays with a monkey and an elephant, jumps around, dances, and swings through the jungle.

She wears really colorful clothes and the song is amazing. It's so exciting! Check it out! You'll love it!

B **IN CLASS** **Talk with a partner.** Read your music video review in **A**.

Vocabulary Focus

A Complete the crossword puzzle.

Down

1.

2.

3.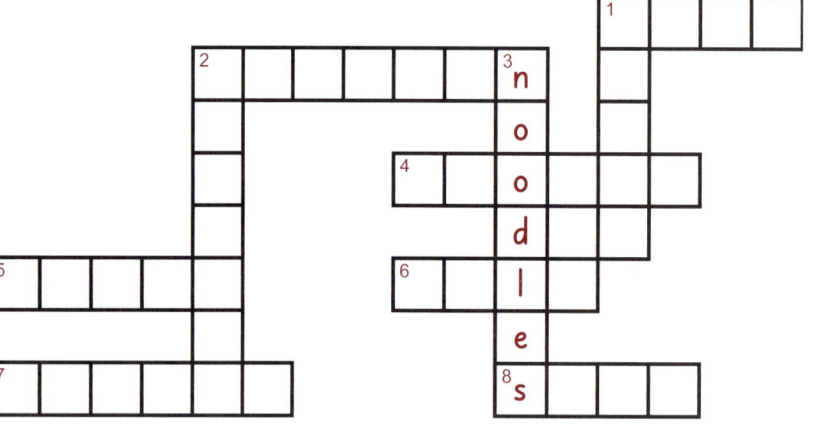

Across

1.

2.

4.

5.

6.

7.

8.

Crossword — Down 3 spells "noodles": n o o d l e s

B Unscramble the words.

1. n k i s   _ _ n _

2. b a l t e   _ _ b _ _

3. n o u c r e t _ _ _ _ n _ _ _ _

4. a t r o g r i e f r e _ _ _ _ r _ _ _ _ _ _ _ _

C Complete the chart. Use the words in the box.

glass	plate	fork	knife	cup	bowl	spoon

THINGS YOU EAT FROM	THINGS TO EAT WITH	THINGS TO PUT DRINKS IN
plate		

Conversation

Complete the conversation. Put the sentences in the correct order.
IN CLASS Practice with a partner.

a. _____ Hey, Izzy! I'm fine, thanks. Are you coming to my birthday party tomorrow?

b. __5__ Cupcakes and ice cream! Great! Do you need anything else?

c. _____ That all sounds great. I can't wait! See you tomorrow.

d. __1__ Hi, Diego! How are you?

e. _____ No, that's OK. We also have burgers, fruit, and cookies.

f. _____ Thanks! We can eat them with ice cream.

g. _____ Yeah, and Sandra's coming, too. We're making cupcakes for you.

Language Focus

A **Complete the conversation.** Circle the correct words.
IN CLASS Practice with two partners.

Katy: Let's have burgers for lunch.

Jeff: OK. . . . Excuse me. Do you have (**any** / **some**) burgers?

Seller: I'm sorry. There (**are** / **aren't**) any left today.

Jeff: Oh, OK. Do you have (**some** / **any**) pizzas?

Seller: Yes. How many do you want?

Katy: Two, please. How about (**any** / **some**) salad, Jeff?

Jeff: Sounds great. . . . Can we have (**any** / **some**) potato salad, please?

Seller: I'm sorry. There (**isn't** / **aren't**) any left. Would you like the pasta salad?

Katy: Yes, please.

B **Complete the questions and answers.**
IN CLASS Practice with a partner.

1. Maria: _____ there _____ vegetables in the refrigerator?

   Ben: No, _____ .

2. Diego: _____ there _____ rice in the cabinet?

   Sofia: No, there _____ , but there's _____ on the counter.

3. Jenny: _____ there _____ plates in the sink?

   Sam: Yes, _____ .

4. Jack: Let's have dessert. _____ there _____ ice cream?

   Ying: No, _____ , but there _____ cookies
   on the table.

5. Ana: _____ there _____ salad on the table?

   Luka: Yes, _____ .

The Real World

Complete the article. Use the words in the box.

> popular   ate   see   senses   sight   table

Chefs usually spend a lot of time making food look—not just taste—good, but what if you (1) _____ food without seeing it first?

Dark dining is a different way to eat food. It happens in a dark restaurant and you do not (2) _____ the food you eat. You choose the type of meal—vegetarian, fish, meat, or a mixture—and guess the foods after the meal.

One restaurant, Dans Le Noir, describes how dark dining is different. The main idea is that when you can't see the food, our other four (3) _____ —taste, smell, touch, and hearing—increase. In Dans Le Noir, you sit at a long (4) _____ , but don't see who you sit next to. This means getting to know people in an unusual way—in the dark. Many dark dining restaurants also support people with (5) _____ problems. People who are blind or have lost a lot of their sight often work in these restaurants.

The first dark dining restaurant opened in 1999 in Zurich, Switzerland. Now, dark dining is (6) _____ around the world. There are restaurants in many places, such as London, New York, Barcelona, Seoul, and Singapore.

Reading

A **Look at the text messages.**
Where is Min-Hee?

    a. at school

    b. at home

    c. at a store

B **Complete the diagram.**

FOOD THEY NEED	NON-FOOD ITEMS THEY NEED	FOOD THEY HAVE

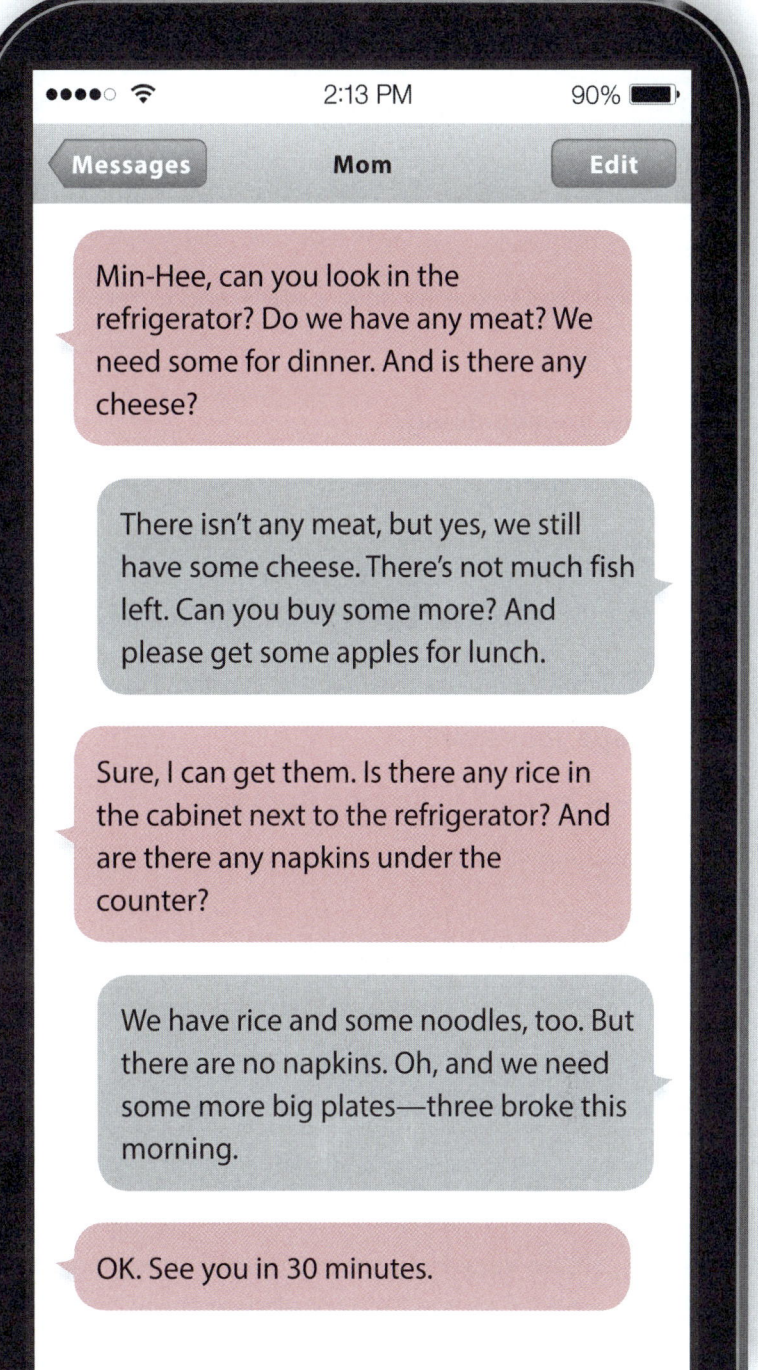

Messages   Mom   **Edit**

Min-Hee, can you look in the refrigerator? Do we have any meat? We need some for dinner. And is there any cheese?

There isn't any meat, but yes, we still have some cheese. There's not much fish left. Can you buy some more? And please get some apples for lunch.

Sure, I can get them. Is there any rice in the cabinet next to the refrigerator? And are there any napkins under the counter?

We have rice and some noodles, too. But there are no napkins. Oh, and we need some more big plates—three broke this morning.

OK. See you in 30 minutes.

C **Answer the questions.**
IN CLASS Talk with a partner.

1. In your family, who usually goes shopping for food?

    _____

2. How often do you go shopping for food?

    _____

Writing

WRITING TIP **Using informal and semi-formal writing**

Use informal and semi-formal writing for different things.

Informal

For writing blogs, text messages, emails, and letters to friends and close family.

> **Hey Vera!**
>
> **How are you doing?**
>
> **Speak soon!**

Semi-formal

For writing school reports, homework, letters, and emails to people you don't know well.

> **Dear Vera,**
>
> **I hope you're well.**
>
> **I look forward to hearing from you.**

A **Write an informal email.** Read the email from Vera and write about a popular food in your country.

From: Vera   **Subject:** Popular Foods

Hi! I'm Vera. How are you doing? I'm doing a project on popular foods around the world. Can you help me answer these questions?

- What's one popular food in your country?

- Where's the best place to eat it?

- How often do you eat it?

- Do you make it at home? What's in it?

B **IN CLASS** **Talk with a partner.** Read your email in **A**.

YOU SHOULD SEE A DOCTOR!

Vocabulary Focus

A **Label the picture.** Use the words in the box.

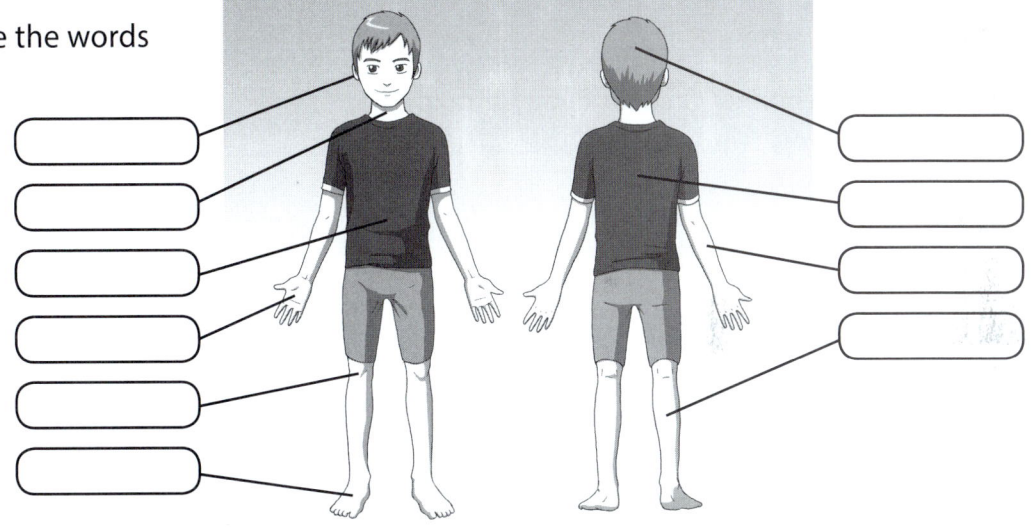

back	ear
arm	throat
leg	head
foot	knee
stomach	hand

B **Complete the chart.** Use the words from **A**. You will use some words twice.

WORDS WITH *ACHE*	WORDS WITH *SORE*

C **Unscramble the words.**

1. l h a e h t _ e _ _ _ _ _

2. o c t d r o _ _ c _ _ _

3. c d i m i n e e _ _ _ i _ _ _ _

4. k b a e r _ _ e _ _

5. k c i s _ _ _ k

6. u h c g o c _ _ _ _ _

Conversation

Complete the conversation. Put the words in the correct order to make sentences.
IN CLASS Practice with a partner.

Nurse: What's wrong with all of you?

Pablo: feel / I don't / a headache / well / and I have

_____.

Nurse: take / wrong / You / some / should / medicine. Kay, what's / with you

_____?

Kay: cut / knee / I / my

_____.

Nurse: for a little / back here again / while. Pat, why are you / OK, / rest here

_____?

Pat: a stomachache / I still feel / I have / really sick, and

_____.

Nurse: go home / Oh dear, / you / should

_____.

Language Focus

A **Complete the sentences.**

1. Jerry broke his arm. What should he _____ ?

2. May and Brian _____ stomachaches. _____ they take some medicine?

3. Sam: I _____ my hand.

   Lucy: Playing tennis isn't a good idea.
   _____ don't you stay home today?

4. Kelly doesn't feel well. She _____
   go to her piano lesson today. It's better
   for her to rest.

5. Donna _____ sick.
   _____ she go to school
   today?

B Correct one mistake on each line.

(IN CLASS) Practice with a partner.

1. Isla: What wrong?

   Luka: I am having a sore throat.

2. Chris: My ear hurt. What should I do?

   Ying: You should staying home.

3. Jack: I have stomachaches.

   Kim: Why do you go to the doctor?

4. Alan: Lisa and Tina both has coughs.

   Peng: Why doesn't they take some medicine?

The Real World

When you hear the word "bacteria," what do you think of? Many people think of diseases and sickness, but there are also some good ways to use bacteria.

The beautiful paintings in Santos Juanes Church in Valencia, Italy, are old—over 300 years old—and some of the paintings are damaged. For example, some parts of the paintings have turned white, while other parts have glue on them.

To clean the paintings, restorers used a special bacteria. This bacteria "eats" the damaged parts without hurting the paintings. After 90 minutes, the special bacteria dries, and the paintings are cleaned. Biologist Pilar Bosch Roig said, "It's quick . . . and it's cheaper than traditional ways."

Read the article. Circle **T** for True or **F** for False.

1. The paintings in Santos Juanes Church are over 900 years old.　　T　F

2. There was glue on some parts of the paintings.　　T　F

3. A "restorer" helps to fix something that is damaged.　　T　F

4. Using bacteria is cheaper than older ways of cleaning paintings.　　T　F

Reading

A **Look at the article.** Where do you usually see these letters?

    a. in a book   b. in a magazine   c. in a report

 ☆ ☆ ☆ ASK AMY! ☆ ☆ ☆

Dear Amy,

Help me! I get colds all winter—one after the other. I had a cold six weeks ago, then another last month, and now I have a cold again! I'm tired of it! What should I do? I like school, and I don't want to stay home every time I have a cold.

Thank you,
Marissa

Dear Marissa,

I'm sorry to hear you have a cold. You should go to your doctor for some medicine. You should also drink lots of water. Eat lots of fruits and vegetables all the time so you don't get more colds.

You can give other people your cold, so you should also stay home and get some rest. That way, you'll get healthy faster and other people won't get sick.

Get well soon,

Amy

Dear Amy,

I eat lunch and drink soda in the cafeteria every day during the week. There are lots of choices, but I don't know what is best. I'm always really hungry after school. I want to eat better lunches so I'm not hungry before dinner. Can you give me some advice?

Thank you,
Fabio

Dear Fabio,

It's great that you want to eat better. Here are some suggestions:

You should eat fruits and vegetables at least twice a day, so try to have some at lunch.

Many cafeterias have pizza and ice cream, but you shouldn't eat junk food more than once a week.

Make sure you drink lots of water. Too much soda or juice is not good for you.

You should also try and get enough calcium. Calcium is in milk products, and it keeps your bones healthy. For example, you can eat cheese or yogurt, or drink milk.

Stay healthy!

Amy

B **Read the article.** Answer the questions.

1. Inference Marissa gets at least _____ colds a year.

    a. three   b. six   c. eight

2. Vocabulary The phrase "I'm tired of it" means to be _____ with something.

    a. fed up   b. pleased   c. happy

3. Detail According to Amy, it is better to drink lots of _____ to stay healthy.

    a. water   b. soda   c. juice

4. Detail Amy tells _____ to eat fruit and vegetables.

    a. Marissa   b. Fabio   c. both Marissa and Fabio

5. Detail According to Amy, calcium is in _____ .

    a. milk   b. vegetables   c. bread

C **Answer the questions.**

1. What kinds of healthy food do you eat? _____

2. What else can people do to stay healthy? _____

Writing

WRITING TIP Using *for example*

Use the term **for example** and give extra information to explain ideas.

Calcium is in milk products. For example, milk, cheese, and yoghurt . . .

comma after the term

Milk, cheese, and yoghurt, for example, have a lot of calcium.

commas before and after the term

A **Read the letter.** Use your answers from **C** above and your own ideas to write a reply to Ben.

Hi,

I know that eating good food, for example, fruits and vegetables, is one way to stay healthy. Can you give me some advice on other things I can do?

Thanks,

Ben

B **IN CLASS** **Talk with a partner.** Read your letter in **A**.

I OFTEN SKATE AFTER SCHOOL.

Vocabulary Focus

A **Complete the crossword puzzle.**

Across

1.

4.

6.

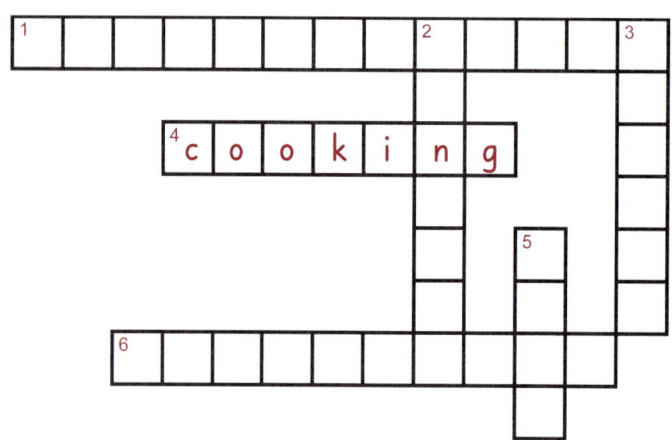

Down

2.

3.

5.

B **Match.** Join the words to their definitions.

1. practice ○   ○ a. on a lower level in a building

2. neighbor ○   ○ b. opposite of quiet

3. downstairs ○   ○ c. person living near you

4. loud ○   ○ d. do something many times to get better

C **Unscramble the words to write how often you do activities.**

1. t o n e f̶   _ f _ _ _ _   4. m̶ o t e s i m e s   _ _ m _ _ _ _ _ _

2. w̶ y s l a a _ _ w _ _ _ _   5. r y h̶ l a d v e r e h _ _ _ _ _ _ _ _ _ _ _ _

3. a t̶ l r e y r _ _ _ _ _ _   6. a l y u̶ s l u   _ _ u _ _ _ _ _

Conversation

Complete the conversation. Put the sentences in the correct order.
IN CLASS Practice with a partner.

a. _____ Oh, hi, Mom. I'm just practicing my guitar.

b. _5_ Hmm . . . well, you should study some more before tomorrow.

c. _____ Why aren't you studying? Don't you have a test tomorrow?

d. _1_ What's all that noise?

e. _____ I do, I'm just taking a break. I already studied for a couple of hours today.

f. _____ OK. Just after this song.

Language Focus

A **Look at the chart.** Answer the questions.
IN CLASS Practice with a partner.

	SATURDAY	SUNDAY
morning	practice the piano	work out
afternoon	always skateboard with friends	1:00 p.m. have lunch with my family usually play tennis
evening	sometimes cook with Mom	always go to the movies

1. What do you do on Saturdays at 10 a.m.? _____

2. What do you do on Saturday afternoons? _____

3. Do you often cook? _____

4. What do you do on Sundays at 11 a.m.? _____

5. What do you usually do on Sunday afternoons? _____

6. Do you often go to the movies? _____

B Correct one mistake in each sentence.

1. I always studying after school.

2. I ever hardly exercise on Fridays.

3. Are you skateboard right now?

4. What do you usually doing on the weekend?

5. I rarely watching TV.

6. I'm exercise right now.

The Real World

Read the article. Complete the chart below.

According to reports, 54% of adults in the United States drink an average of 3 cups of coffee every day. Some experts believe that drinking too much coffee every day is a bad habit and not good for your health. But recent studies show that drinking coffee can have positive benefits. So, is this bad habit actually good for you?

Research by the Harvard Medical School in the U.S. looked at the differences between people who drink coffee and people who don't. People who drink coffee often have cream and sugar in their drinks, which are not healthy. Drinking too much coffee can also cause some people to have headaches and stomachaches, and even cause sleeping problems.

However, the study shows that caffeine—a chemical in coffee—can help the brain function better, and improve your mood. Coffee also contains antioxidants. These help to fight several diseases.

So, is coffee good for you? Research is ongoing, but experts generally agree that a small amount of coffee can be healthy.

REASONS FOR COFFEE	REASONS AGAINST COFFEE

Reading

A **Read the article.** It is mainly about what students do _____.

   a. at the weekends   b. during the weekdays   c. on holidays

JUST A REGULAR DAY

What do you think is a typical day for someone who is 15–19 years old? Do you think students' answers are different in each country? The American Time Use Survey (ATUS) is a study by the Bureau of Labor Statistics. They interviewed American high-school students about their average day.

The ATUS shows that a typical day for American students includes around 8 hours of sleep, 7.5 hours of school, 4 hours of sports or leisure activities, and 4.5 hours of other activities (including travel, activities in the house, and eating). All students spend around two hours a day of their leisure time watching TV. But that's where the similarities end; the amount of time spent on leisure and other activities is different between male and female students.

In an average day, female students spend around one hour socializing, around 30 minutes using a computer or playing video games, and under 30 minutes doing sports. However, male students spend around one hour playing video games and one hour doing sports.

Results from the ATUS also show that driving, part-time work, and doing volunteer work are part of the typical day for some American high-school students.

B **Complete the diagram.** Use information from *Just A Regular Day*.

All Students

1. _____
2. _____
3. _____
Other (travel, eating, activities in the house) — 4.5 hours

A Typical Day

Female Students: Leisure Activity and Time Spent

watch TV — 2 hours
4. _____
5. _____
6. _____

Male Students: Leisure Activity and Time Spent

7. _____
8. _____
sports — 1 hour

C **Answer the questions.**

1. How many hours a day do you sleep and study? _____

2. What do you usually do during your leisure time? _____

Writing

WRITING TIP Apostrophes

Use an apostrophe (') and the letter **s** to show something belongs to someone.

Jack's skateboard is red.

apostrophe

For plurals ending in **s**, put the apostrophe after the **s**.

Do you think students' answers are different in each country?

A **Write an email.** Use your answers from **C** above and your own ideas to write about a typical day for students in your country.

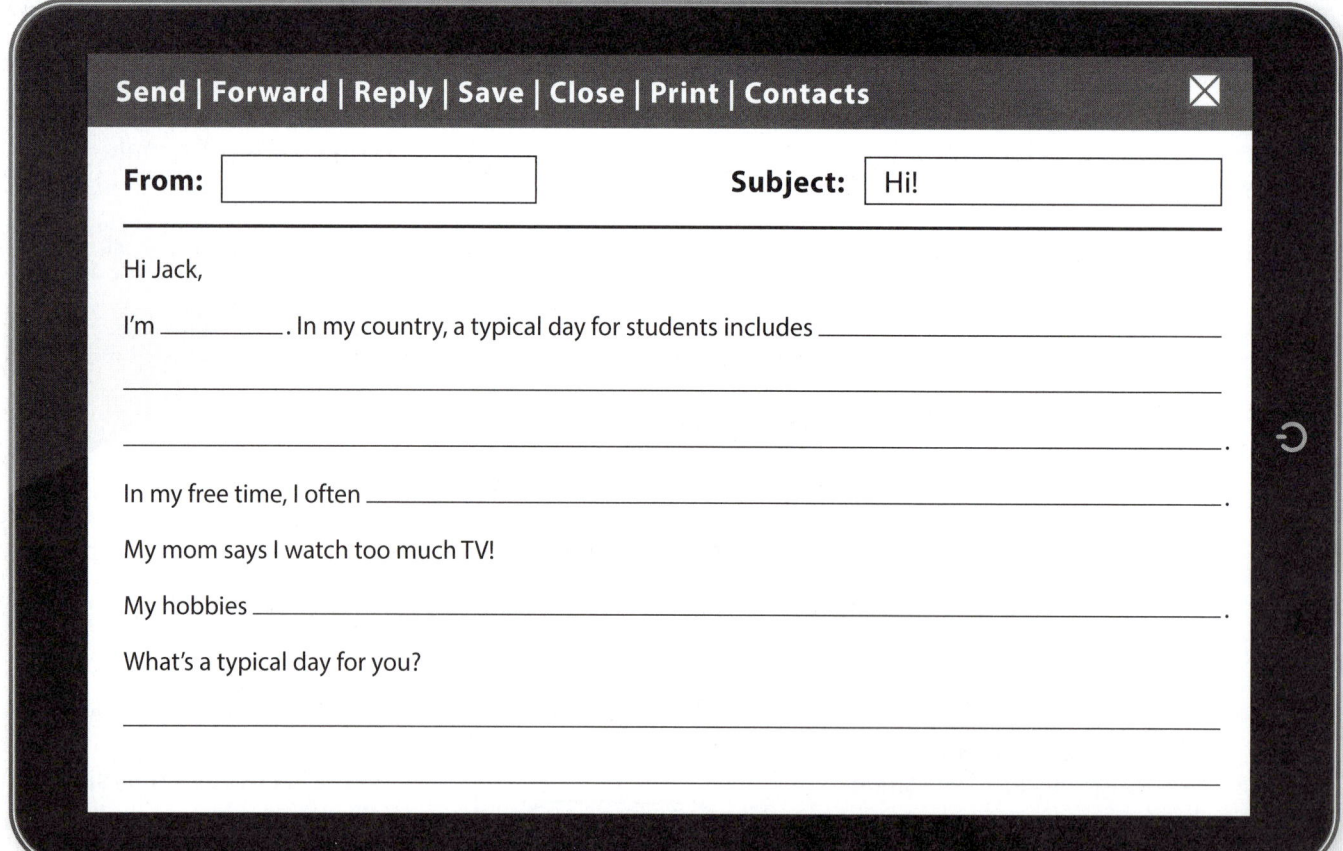

Send | Forward | Reply | Save | Close | Print | Contacts

From: _____   **Subject:** Hi!

Hi Jack,

I'm _____ . In my country, a typical day for students includes _____
_____
_____ .

In my free time, I often _____ .

My mom says I watch too much TV!

My hobbies _____ .

What's a typical day for you?

_____
_____

B **IN CLASS** **Talk with a partner.** Read your email in **A**.

10 HOW DO YOU GET TO THE MALL?

Vocabulary Focus

A **Complete the puzzle.** Use the chart.

1	2	3	4	5	6	7	8	9	10	11	12	13	14	15
a	c	e	h	i	k	m	n	o	p	r	s	t	u	v

1. $\overline{\quad}_{10}\ \overline{\quad}_{1}\ \overline{\quad}\ \overline{\quad}_{6}$

2. $\overline{\quad}_{7}\ \overline{\quad}_{14}\ \overline{\quad}_{12}\ \overline{\quad}\ \overline{\quad}_{14}\ \overline{\quad}_{7}$

3. $\overline{\quad}_{11}\ \overline{\quad}_{3}\ \overline{\quad}_{12}\ \overline{\quad}_{13}\ \overline{\quad}\ \overline{\quad}_{14}\ \overline{\quad}_{11}\ \overline{\quad}_{1}\ \overline{\quad}_{8}\ \overline{\quad}$

4. $\overline{\quad}_{7}\ \overline{\quad}_{9}\ \overline{\quad}\ \overline{\quad}_{5}\ \overline{\quad}_{3}\ \overline{\quad}_{13}\ \overline{\quad}_{4}\ \overline{\quad}_{3}\ \overline{\quad}_{1}\ \overline{\quad}_{13}\ \overline{\quad}_{3}\ \overline{\quad}_{11}$

5. $\overline{\quad}_{12}\ \overline{\quad}_{14}\ \overline{\quad}_{10}\ \overline{\quad}_{3}\ \overline{\quad}_{11}\ \overline{\quad}\ \overline{\quad}_{1}\ \overline{\quad}_{11}\ \overline{\quad}_{6}\ \overline{\quad}_{3}\ \overline{\quad}_{13}$

6. $\overline{\quad}\ \overline{\quad}_{9}\ \overline{\quad}_{8}\ \overline{\quad}_{15}\ \overline{\quad}_{3}\ \overline{\quad}_{8}\ \overline{\quad}_{5}\ \overline{\quad}_{3}\ \overline{\quad}_{8}\ \overline{\quad}_{2}\ \overline{\quad}_{3}$
$\overline{\quad}_{12}\ \overline{\quad}_{13}\ \overline{\quad}_{9}\ \overline{\quad}_{11}\ \overline{\quad}_{3}$

B **Complete the sentences.** Use the words from **A**.

1. You see interesting things in a _____ and you watch a movie in a _____.

2. You go to a _____ to buy food. You sit at a table and eat dinner in a _____.

3. Many people go running and skateboarding in a _____.

4. In a _____, you can often buy things 24 hours a day.

C **Complete the sentences.** Where is the red house (**A**)?

> in front of   behind   on the corner of   next to   between   across from

1. A is _____ B.

2. A is _____ B.

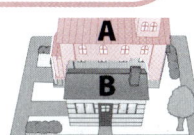
3. A is _____ B.

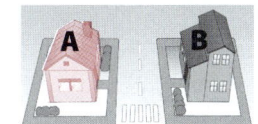
4. A is _____ B.

5. A is _____ B and C.

6. A is _____ 1st and 14th street.

Conversation

Match. Join the two parts of the conversation.

(IN CLASS) Practice with a partner.

1. Excuse me. Can you help me? ○   ○ a. Oh. The mall's on Tenth Street.

2. I want to go to the mall. ○   ○ b. You're welcome.

3. Mmm . . . where's Tenth Street? ○   ○ c. Sure. Where do you want to go?

4. So, straight and then left at ○   ○ d. Go straight down First Avenue and turn
   the corner?   left.

5. Got it. Thanks. ○   ○ e. That's right. The mall is next to the art museum.

Language Focus

A **Complete the conversations.** Use the words in parentheses.

1. Keiko: Excuse me. How do I get to the park?

   Mark: **(straight)** _____

   (past) _____

   (across from) _____

   Keiko: Thanks.

2. Brian: Excuse me. Can you tell me how to get to the shoe store?

   Kim: **(right)** _____

   (left) _____

   (between) _____

   Brian: Thank you.

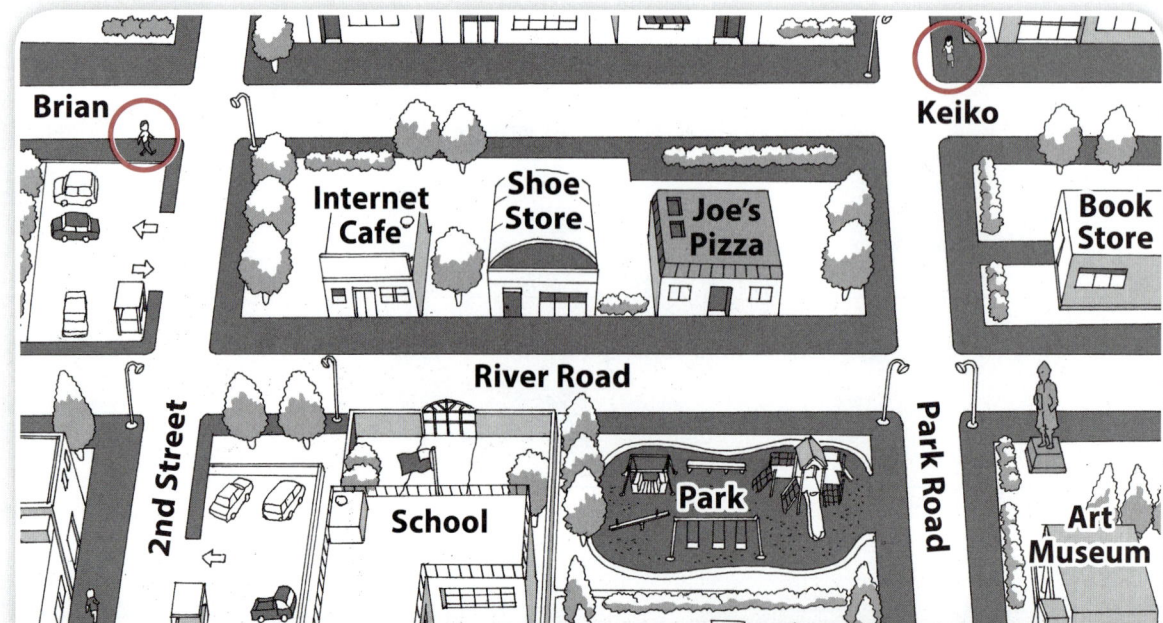

B **Correct one mistake on each line.**

IN CLASS Practice with a partner.

Angela: Excuse me. Can you tell me where the history museum **is**?

Chris: Oh. It's in the corner of Washington Street and Elm Street.

Angela: Umm . . . How do you get to?

Chris: Go straight down this Center Street. Then turn right.

Angela: OK. Down this street and turning right.

Chris: The museum is at the left.

Angela: Thanks you.

The Real World

Read the article. Circle **T** for True or **F** for False.

Daniel Raven-Ellison is a city explorer. He says, "When I travel, I always keep my eyes peeled for unusual . . . art." This type of unusual art is often out on the street, not inside buildings. When Raven-Ellison finds the art, he looks at the surroundings and thinks about why the artist chose that place.

Raven-Ellison also looks at the art itself. He wants to understand what the artist is trying to tell other people. He believes that sometimes the message is playful and amusing, and other times it's beautiful and amazing. Sometimes, the artist may have no message at all.

The art that Raven-Ellison likes the most shows the artist's opinions. He likes it when people can "hear" the message above the noise of the city.

1. To "keep your eyes peeled" means to   **T**   **F**
   look carefully for something.

2. Raven-Ellison looks for art outside on   **T**   **F**
   the streets.

3. He believes the art always has a   **T**   **F**
   message.

4. His favorite art shows the artist's   **T**   **F**
   thoughts and feelings.

Reading

A **Look at the postcard.** Where is Eldora?

    a. New Jersey   b. New Mexico   c. New York

Hi Fran,

New York City is amazing! There are lots of things to see here, but I like Central Park the best. It's right in the middle of the city. It's huge, and the park has a zoo, a theater, and a museum. Millions of people go there each year. Many people walk, bike, or run there in the day.

Yesterday, we went to the park. First, we got on the B train near the Rockefeller Center. I told you about that in my last postcard. The train ride was really interesting because we saw many different kinds of people. We got off at 81st Street. At first we didn't know where to go, and we walked around for a little while. Finally, a nice family helped us, and we were there in no time!

Right now, it's very cold and snowy here. People are ice skating, and it looks cool. I want to try!

See you when I get home next week!

Eldora

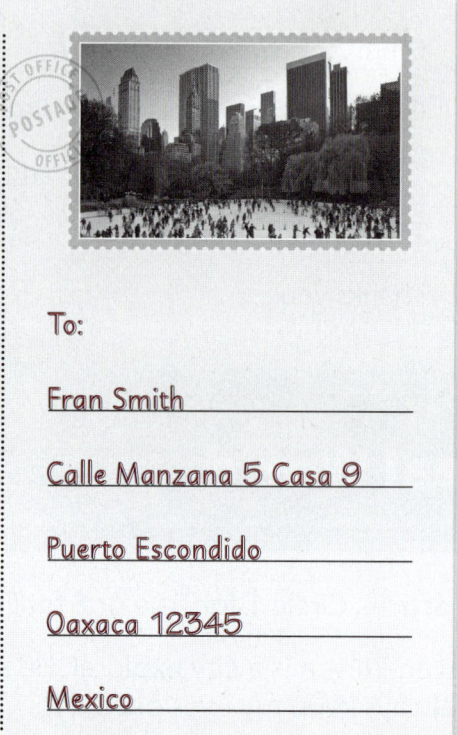

To:

Fran Smith

Calle Manzana 5 Casa 9

Puerto Escondido

Oaxaca 12345

Mexico

B **Read the postcard.** Answer the questions.

1. Main Idea Eldora is _____.

    a. writing a travel book   b. planning a vacation   c. visiting another country

2. Vocabulary The word "huge" means _____.

    a. very big   b. very small   c. medium-sized

3. Detail According to the postcard, there is a theater _____ Central Park.

    a. down the street from   b. inside   c. around the corner from

4. Detail They got off the train at _____.

    a. Rockefeller Center   b. Central Park   c. 81st Street

5. Inference What season was it in New York when Eldora wrote the postcard?

    a. summer   b. fall   c. winter

C **Answer the questions.**

1. What do people do in the park in your city? _____

2. Which is the best museum in your city? _____

Writing

WRITING TIP **Using words to give steps**

Use the words below to help explain the order when giving directions.

First / **The first step is . . .**

Second / **Third**

Then / **After that** / **Later**

Before / **After**

Lastly / **Finally** / **The last step is . . .**

First, take the train to Elm Street. **Then**, turn right before the park, and turn left at the corner of Maple Street. **The last step is** to go past the market and **after that** is the museum.

A **Complete the chart.** Use your own answers.

	PLACE NAME	REASONS TO VISIT
Favorite place to eat		
Favorite place to shop		

B **Write a short paragraph.** Use your answers from **A** and give directions from your school to your favorite places. Give reasons to visit these places.

_____

_____

_____

_____

_____

_____

C **IN CLASS** **Talk with a partner.** Read your paragraph in **B**.

WHAT WERE YOU DOING?

Vocabulary Focus

A **Look at the numbers.** Match the numbers to the letters to make words.

1	2	3	4	5	6	7	8	9	10	11	12	13	14	15
a	b	c	d	e	i	n	o	r	s	t	u	v	x	y

1. __ __ __ __ __ __ __ __
   1 4 13   7 11 12 9 5

2. __ __ __ __ __
   2   1 13 5

3. __ __ __ __
   11 6 9   4

4. __ __ __ __ __ __ __
   5 14 3 6 11   4

5. __ __ __ __ __ __ __
      3 3 6 4 5 7 11

6. __ __ __ __ __ __ __
   7 5 9 13 8 12

B **Complete the phrases.** Circle the correct words.

1. (**set** / **turn**) an alarm

2. (**feel** / **see**) an accident

3. take (**a risk** / **an experience**)

4. be (**excitement** / **excited**)

C **Match.** Join the two words or phrases with the same meaning.

1. not sleeping ○ ○ oversleep

2. ask for food in a restaurant ○ ○ jog

3. not wake up when you should ○ ○ order

4. run slowly ○ ○ ring

5. what the phone does when ○ ○ awake
   someone calls us

Conversation

Complete the conversation. Put the sentences in the correct order.

IN CLASS Practice with a partner.

a. _____ They sure are! Then we went diving. We were looking at all these little fish when a ray swam past us. Later we saw a huge turtle and a baby shark, too.

b. _____ A ray and a shark! I hope I can try scuba diving some day!

c. _____ That's awesome! Dolphins are such beautiful animals.

d. _____ Yeah. The excitement started before we were even in the water. We saw dolphins on the boat ride out to the dive.

e. _____ I sure did! I went scuba diving. It was really cool!

f. _1_ I heard you had an amazing vacation.

g. _____ Scuba diving? Wow! Was it your first time?

Language Focus

A **Correct one mistake in each sentence.**

1. I am skateboarding when I fell over.

2. We were have a barbeque when the fireworks started.

3. I was still in bed when the phone ringing.

4. I was jogging was I saw the famous movie star!

5. I was going home when the snow start.

6. I finish the test when the bell rang.

B **Complete the sentences.** Write the correct forms of the verbs.

1. I _____ (**ride**) my skateboard when I _____ (**break**) my arm.

2. My brother _____ (**jog**) in the park when the storm _____ (**start**).

3. My parents _____ (**walk**) on the beach when they _____ (**see**) a dolphin in the ocean.

4. She _____ (**climb**) the mountain when she _____ (**fall**) and cut her leg.

5. He _____ (**hike**) in the rain forest when he suddenly _____ (**hear**) a bird singing.

The Real World

Read the article. Answer the questions.

When you think of coral, what do you imagine? Colorful coral in shallow tropical reefs, like Australia's Great Barrier Reef? While most coral live in these places, there are some—like the ones Rhian Waller studies—living in very different places.

Deep sea coral live far below the surface—sometimes as far as 2,000 meters down—in cold water (about 4°C). There is no sunlight that far down, and the coral grow much more slowly than on tropical reefs—some reefs grow only one millimeter a year.

Because these deep sea coral live so far down, scientists find it difficult to study them. The first time they could see these coral properly was in the late 1970s, in small submarines. However, even though these coral are so far down, they are still in danger. Deep sea fishing, submarine communication cables, and exploring for oil and gas are destroying reefs in some areas. It is important that scientists continue to research these special coral, to learn how we can help protect them.

1. Deep sea coral can live up to _____ meters below the surface.

   a. 2,000   b. 4,000   c. 8,000

2. Tropical coral grows _____ deep sea coral.

   a. slower than

   b. at the same rate as

   c. faster than

3. Scientists first visited deep sea coral in the late _____.

   a. 1950s   b. 1970s   c. 1990s

4. It's important for scientists to continue researching the coral to _____ them.

   a. find   b. collect   c. look after

Reading

A **Look at the photo.** What do you think the article is about?

a. base jumping   b. snowboarding   c. climbing

UP IN THE MOUNTAINS

Gerlinde Kaltenbrunner is an extraordinary mountain climber. She has climbed 14 of the world's highest mountains, which are all over 8,000 meters high. Because the air is thinner, most climbers need extra oxygen to reach the top of these mountains. However, Kaltenbrunner is the first woman to climb all 14 mountains without extra oxygen.

Kaltenbrunner started climbing when she was growing up in the mountains in Austria. At 13 years old, she climbed her first big mountain, Sturzhahn at 2,028 meters high. She became a nurse, but always had a passion for climbing. At 32 years old, Kaltenbrunner climbed her fourth major mountain—Nanga Parbat in Pakistan—and decided to become a full-time mountain climber.

In 2007, Kaltenbrunner had an accident while climbing Dhaulagiri in Nepal—the world's seventh highest mountain. She was inside her tent one morning when an avalanche struck. When the avalanche stopped, it was very dark and she didn't know where she was. She had a small knife, and cut a hole in the tent. Slowly, Kaltenbrunner managed to get out of the deep snow and to the surface.

Kaltenbrunner recovered from the accident. "I couldn't stop climbing," she says. "This is my life. A year later I returned to the same spot. There was the most beautiful sunrise I have ever seen." She climbed the 14th mountain—K2 between Pakistan and China—in 2011. Although she has climbed through deep snow, freezing temperatures, and dangerous rockfalls, Kaltenbrunner says she feels quite safe most of the time. "The most important thing is to have passion inside," she says. "If you really love something, you'll find a way to reach it."

B **Read the article.** Circle **T** for True or **F** for False.

1. Kaltenbrunner has climbed 15 of the world's highest mountains.   T   F

2. It is more difficult to breathe at the top of the world's highest mountains.   T   F

3. A "passion" is a strong interest in something.   T   F

4. Kaltenbrunner had an accident while climbing in Pakistan.   T   F

5. Kaltenbrunner was outside when the avalanche struck.   T   F

6. Although there are risks, Kaltenbrunner enjoys climbing mountains.   T   F

C **Write.** Correct the false sentences in **B**.

_____

_____

_____

Writing

WRITING TIP Using *although*

Use **although** to join two short sentences. Writers use **although** to tell readers they are surprised or they think something is unusual.

Although she has climbed through deep snow, freezing temperatures, and dangerous rockfalls, Kaltenbrunner says she feels quite safe most of the time.

tells us a result that is surprising
(climbing is dangerous but she feels quite safe most of the time)

A **Write a short paragraph about an adventure you had.** Use *although*.

_____

_____

_____

_____

_____

B **IN CLASS** **Talk with a partner.** Read your paragraph in **A**.

12

WE'RE GOING TO VOLUNTEER!

Vocabulary Focus

A Unscramble the words about volunteering and charity events.

1. s e i r a   _ _a_ _ _ _

2. e o t d a n   _ _o_ _ _ _ _ _

3. r a h t s   _ _r_ _ _ _

4. o z a r i g e n   _ _ _ _a_ _ _ _ _

5. l e p n u a c   _ _ _ _a_ _ _ _

6. u a r f i d s r e n   _ _ _ _ _ _ _ _ _e_ _

B **Complete the sentences.** Use the words from **A**.

1. We're going to pick up ＿＿＿＿＿ at the beach.

2. I'm going to help ＿＿＿＿＿ a school fair.

3. Let's have a concert as a ＿＿＿＿＿ for charity.

4. I want to ＿＿＿＿＿ warm clothes to people in the winter.

5. I'm going to help ＿＿＿＿＿ and put things away after the event.

6. We want to ＿＿＿＿＿ money for new band uniforms so we're selling cakes.

C **Complete the phrases.** Circle the correct words.

1. put up (**decorations** / **trash**)

2. have a (**volunteer** / **fundraiser**)

3. (**raise** / **organize**) money

4. (**donate** / **bake**) books

Conversation

Complete the conversation. Put the words in the correct order to make sentences.

IN CLASS Practice with two partners.

Peng: people / How / are / come / to / many / going / the / to / party

_____?

Bella: think / About / I / thirty _____.

Peng: OK, thirty is good. Where are we going to have it?

Tom: in / have / gym / the / it / Let's _____.

Peng: decorate / gym / going / to / the / Who's _____?

Bella: I am, and Todd's going to help me.

Tom: going / food / to / get / I'm / the _____.

Peng: The party is going to be great! I can't wait!

Language Focus

A **Look at the chart.** Complete the questions and answers.

IN CLASS Practice with a partner.

FUNDRAISER SCHEDULE—10 DAYS UNTIL THE EVENT		
Before next Monday	Find volunteers to sing and play music	Matt, Andie, Paul
Morning of the event	Put up decorations	Lee, Becky
At the event	Collect money	Stacy
After the event	Pick up trash	Jamie, Amanda

1. When is the charity event? ___It's ten days from now._____

2. Is Paul going to clean up after the fundraiser? _____

3. Who's going to find volunteers? _____

4. What are Lee and Becky going to do for the event? _____

5. _____ Yes, she is. She's doing it by herself.

6. _____ Jamie and Amanda are.

B **Look at the chart on page 60.** Correct one mistake on each line.

1. The fundraiser was the week after next.

2. Who's going to finding volunteers?

3. When are they go to put up decorations?

4. Are they going collect money?

5. Stacy's go to collect money.

6. They are going to picked up trash after the event.

The Real World

Read the article. Circle the correct answers.

Look at the chart. The number of people living on Earth is increasing all the time. What does this mean for the food we all need?

First, to grow extra food for the increasing population, we are going to use more natural resources like oil and water. Second, we are going to need more land for all those people's houses. That means we are going to have fewer places to grow food. There may not be enough food for everyone.

However, today we waste about one-third of the world's food. If we want to feed the increasing population, we shouldn't wait to try to solve these problems. We should start being careful now. Here are some simple things you can do: first, don't waste resources—don't buy more food than you need; second, save food you don't eat for another meal. Every little bit helps!

WORLD POPULATION	
1980	4,449,049,000
1990	5,320,817,000
2000	6,127,000,000
2010	6,916,183,000
2020 (estimate)	7,716,749,000
2030 (estimate)	8,424,937,000

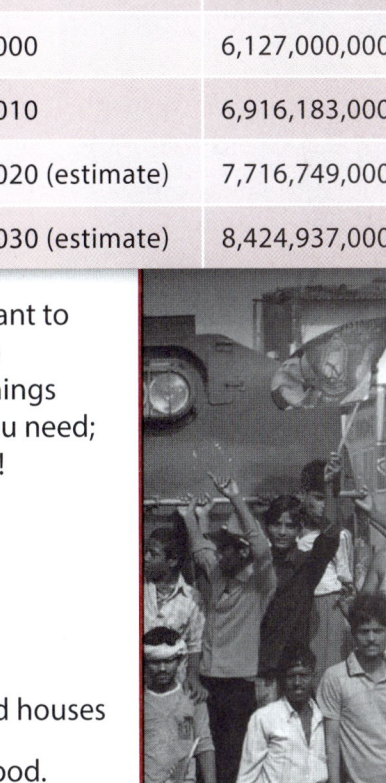

1. The world's population passed 6 billion people in _____.

   a. the 1980s   b. the 1990s   c. the 2000s

2. Which are examples of natural resources?

   a. fruits and vegetables   b. water and oil   c. gardens and houses

3. In the future, we are going to need more water and _____ to grow food.

   a. land   b. oil   c. people

4. The author believes many people _____.

   a. should go shopping
      more often
   b. buy more food
      than they can eat
   c. don't buy enough
      food

Reading

A **Read the article.** What's another title for this article?

a. Feeding the World   b. Bad Bacteria   c. Growing Food Slowly

REDUCING
WORLD HUNGER

When most people think of bacteria, they think they are bad—and they often are. However, in 2014, three high-school students from Ireland found a new, good way to use bacteria to help grow more food. The three girls—Ciara Judge, Émer Hickey, and Sophie Healy-Thow—are interested in how science can help feed the Earth's growing population.

One day, Hickey's mother was in her garden, and noticed something on the roots of her pea plants. The girls learned that pea plants have lumps on their roots containing a kind of bacteria called Diazotroph. The Diazotroph bacteria help the peas grow faster. So, the girls decided to test it with other kinds of plants.

As an experiment, they added the bacteria to barley seeds. They repeated the experiment many times, and found the plants started growing in half as much time, and produced up to 30% more food than normal plants.

The girls are going to continue their research to see if the bacteria can also help other kinds of food plants. They say they take "a great interest in how the world works and how we can help those around us."

B **Read the article again.** Circle **T** for True or **F** for False.

1. The three students are from Ireland.   **T**   **F**

2. The goal of the students' research is to grow more food for the world.   **T**   **F**

3. The pea plants had lumps on their leaves.   **T**   **F**

4. The students added the Diazotroph to barley.   **T**   **F**

5. During the experiment, the plants produced over 40% more food   **T**   **F**
   than normal plants.

C Answer the questions.

1. Name one world problem you think about. _____

2. What's one thing you can do to help the problem? _____

Writing

WRITING TIP **Using *so***

Use the word **so** to join two sentences, and to say "for that reason" or show a result.

reason

Their plants grew faster than normal plants, so the students think this is going to help us in the future.

result

A **Write a short report.** Use your answers from **C** above and your own ideas to write about a world problem and what you can do to help.

B **IN CLASS** **Talk with a partner.** Read your report in **A**.

Photo Credits

1 John Coletti/JAI/Corbis, **3** EschCollection/Getty Images, **4** Mike Hutchings/Reuters, **5** Radius Images/Getty Images, **6** The Washington Post/Getty Images, **7** Essdras M Suarez/Boston Globe/Getty Images, **9** Jamie Grill/Getty Images, **10** Jose Luis Pelaez Inc./Getty Images, **11** 4X-image/Getty Images, **12** Nicolas Russell/Getty Images, **14** Glow Images/Getty Images, **16** DAJ/Getty Images, **17** Image Source/Getty Images, **19** Tom Murphy/NGC, **20** Digital Vision/Thinkstock, **21** Wu Swee Ong/Getty Images, **22** Design Pics Inc./NGC, **24** Cultura RM/Jakob Helbig/Getty Images, **25** (c) Paul Nicklen/NGC, (b) Simo Graells/Shutterstock, **26** Mark Bowler/Getty Images, **27** Stefan Christmann/Terra/Corbis, **29** Jason Bahr/Bud Light/Getty Images, **30** Joseph Okpako/Getty Images, **31** Gary Burchell/Getty Images, **32** DEA/A. Dagli Orti/Getty Images, **34** Robert Nicholas/Getty Images, **35** Fuse/Getty Images, **36** Jason Redmond/Reuters, **39** Ariel Skelley/Blend/Corbis, **40** 68/Ocean/Corbis, **41** Manuel Bruque/Corbis Wire/Corbis, **42** Jason Stitt/Shutterstock, **44** Michael Nichols/NGC, **46** (t) Tom Merton/Getty Images, (b) Shuji Kobayashi/Getty Images, **47** UpperCut Images/Alamy, **49** Ken Seet/Cardinal/Corbis, **51** Mario Anzuoni/Reuters, **52** Alan Copson/Passage/Corbis, **54** Montico Lionel/Terra/Corbis, **55** PeopleImages.com/Getty Images, **56** George Grall/NGC, **57** Tommy Heinrich/NGC, **59** Hero Images/Corbis, **61** Krishna Murari Kishan/Reuters, **62** AP Images/Niall Carson

NGC = National Geographic Creative

Art Credits

9 Z-art/Shutterstock, Kynata/Shutterstock, Anna Marynenko/Shutterstock, **14** Hein Nouwens/Shutterstock, Andromina/Shutterstock, Reamolko/Shutterstock, **14, 44** Bioraven/Shutterstock, **34** Chistoprudnaya/Shutterstock, cheesekerbs/Shutterstock, Goldenarts/Shutterstock, TsipiLevin/Shutterstock, Justone/Shutterstock, **39, 49, 50** Gaim Creative Studio, **44** Aliaksandr Radzko/Shutterstock, VitaminCo/Shutterstock, Snorks/Shutterstock